TRULY
KNOWN

TRULY
KNOWN

Devotions of God's
Grace in Our Lives

REDEMPTION
PRESS

JAYNE MARTIN PATTON

Cover design by Courtney Longnecker

Published by Redemption Press, PO Box 427, Enumclaw, WA 98022.

Toll-Free (844) 2REDEEM (273-3336)

Redemption Press is honored to present this title in partnership with the author. The views expressed or implied in this work are those of the author. Redemption Press provides our imprint seal representing design excellence, creative content, and high-quality production.

ISBN: 978-1-68314-857-9 (Paperback)
978-1-68314-858-6 (ePub)
978-1-68314-859-3 (Mobi)

Library of Congress Catalog Card Number: 2020902943

DEDICATION

WITHOUT A DOUBT, THIS LITTLE GATHERING of daily devotions must be dedicated to my parents, Dr. Dave and Terry Martin. Without them raising me up in the Lord, praying for me as a prodigal, loving me back into the fold, challenging me to go deeper with Jesus, and encouraging me to pursue all that God has for me, I don't know that I would be who I am today. There are no words in the English language to express my eternal gratitude for their support. Dad and Mom, I love you both. Thank you for loving Jesus and sharing His love with others so well.

CONTENTS

INTRODUCTION

IN 2017 MUSICIAN TAUREN WELLS WROTE and performed the song "Known." The lyrics ministered to me in such a powerful way. The words reminded me that everything I had ever wanted to keep hidden about myself was already fully known by God. Not only did He know everything about me, He was choosing to love me anyway. The song went on to say that God's grace was ridiculous. I can certainly agree with that, especially as it related to me and my past.

By definition, *ridiculous* means "deserving or inviting derision or mockery; absurd." When partnered with the biblical understanding of God's grace (unmerited favor), it basically means that God should be mocked for extending His grace to sinners like you, and me. But the thing is, God doesn't agree with that assessment.

He doesn't think His grace toward us is ridiculous at all. Why? Because He delights in loving us. Enjoys having us as His children. Rushes in to save us when we've made a terrible mess of things. The fact that we are fully known and loved by God in spite of all our flaws and failings is an inexplicable expression of His powerful, purposeful, and completely ridiculous grace!

Being a recipient of God's ridiculous grace has drastically changed my life. I've gone from trying to find my place of belonging in a world that has proven to be fickle in its acceptance to knowing I'm a welcomed member of the family of God. I no longer need man's approval because I've come to understand what it is to have God's approval. I want to spend the rest of my life telling others—you—how much He fully knows and loves you too, as ridiculous as that may sound.

Friend, you won't find deep theological writings in between these pages. My goal is to make some of the harder truths found in Scripture more understandable to the common, finite mind and heart. I don't write as someone who knows all the answers but rather as someone who is ready to come alongside and cheer you on in your daily walk with Jesus. If you garner just a little bit of encouragement from these devotional words, I will be thrilled. May the Lord continue to be glorified in all of our lives!

WHEN LIFE SHATTERS

*The Spirit of the Lord is upon me, for he has anointed
me to bring Good News to the poor. He has sent me to
proclaim that captives will be released, that the blind will
see, that the oppressed will be set free.*

Luke 4:18 NLT

A WOMAN SAT ACROSS FROM ME in a local coffee shop, spewing out her shattered heart, pleading for hope. She had discovered a love letter from her husband's mistress in his briefcase while helping him find some important paperwork. I didn't know what to say, so I silently began asking Jesus to minister to her heart in this desperate situation.

The Greek word for *oppressed*, used only once in Scripture, means "crushed or shattered in pieces." Whether it's the shattered dream of a flawless marriage, an ideal childhood, a perfect family, impeccable friendships, or even maintaining an unshakeable faith, at some point, many of us have found ourselves trying to glue together the broken pieces of a shattered life.

This passage helps us to remember that Jesus came to heal

our shattered, oppressed hearts. Though we did not choose to be shattered, we can choose to take those broken pieces to Jesus and receive His healing today.

In what ways have you seen Jesus's redemptive character at work in your life-shattering experience?

AFTER TWELVE YEARS

A woman in the crowd had suffered for twelve years with constant bleeding, and she could find no cure. Coming up behind Jesus, she touched the fringe of his robe. Immediately, the bleeding stopped.

Luke 8:43–44 NLT

I RECEIVED A TEXT IN THE middle of the night from a sweet girl who had recently suffered a great loss. It read, "I have a Bible. Where do I start?" Even in her vast sense of emptiness, she understood that somehow comfort would be found among that sacred text. She had recognized that she needed more than what this world could offer her.

Through this I was reminded of the woman, in the book of Luke, who was suffering from a hemorrhage for twelve years. In this story she deliberately worked her way through the crowd to touch the hem of Jesus's robe as He walked through her town.

It was her hopeful faith that brought her to the Healer. In response to this, He not only healed her but sent her away filled with peace. I tend to think He knew she needed her peace of mind restored as much as her physical healing, as the years of searching for healing had probably left her emotionally, physically, and spiritually exhausted. I'm grateful to be reminded through this story that God knows exactly what we need. Only a good God will send us away with more than we've asked for when we come to Him for help.

You might wonder how I advised my midnight texter. I told her to do exactly what the woman in this story did. To reach out to Jesus deliberately and ask Him to heal her heart, her mind, and her body because that is the kind of healing my friend needed. I'm grateful that's the kind of healing Jesus still brings today.

Has your faith ever brought you to Christ with a specific need? What does it look like for you to deliberately reach out to Jesus for healing?

WHEN JESUS QUALIFIES YOU

The names of the twelve apostles are these: first, Simon,
who is called Peter, and Andrew his brother; James the son
of Zebedee, and John his brother.
Matthew 10:2 ESV

HAVE YOU EVER QUESTIONED GOD'S CHOICE in using you or doubted your qualifications for the things God has called you to do? You are in good company!

Peter was erratic and opinionated, often claiming allegiance to Jesus and then denying even knowing Him during his arrest. James and John had fiery tempers. All of them lacked formal education and were highly judgmental of those who were not like them.

If three of Jesus's disciples, His inner circle, all brought their idiosyncrasies to the table, and Jesus still chose them, then rest assured He knew what He was doing when He chose you. Jesus has a way of seeing beyond our glaring imperfections and seeing the extraordinary potential of what He can do through our lives.

Jesus didn't pursue us because of our perfection but rather because of His. We would be wise not to disqualify ourselves when He Himself has told us that He alone is all the qualification we need.

Have you ever found yourself disqualifying yourself before you step out in faith? How has Jesus revealed to you that you are indeed the one He has qualified for such a calling?

CRAZY TRANSFORMATION

But I tell you the truth, no prophet is accepted
in his hometown.
Luke 4:24 NLT

YOUR FAMILY THINKS YOU'RE CRAZY. YOUR circle of friends has been decreasing in size. Not too long ago, you gave your life to Jesus and things have changed rapidly. The dreams and desires you previously had for your life have been replaced by God's. You can't even explain exactly what's been happening, simply because you're not the same person you were before your encounter with Jesus. Truly, your heart has been transformed.

So why the resistance from your friends and family to embrace this new you? Often times when you step out in faith to do what you believe God has called you to do, the people you grew up with will be the first to question it. The reality is that the people you grew up with will continue to harbor memories of your former self. They may prefer to reminisce about who you used to be than to give credence to who you are becoming.

I am reassured by this passage in Luke that reveals when Jesus showed up in His boyhood home of Nazareth, they asked one another, "Isn't this Joseph's son?" This wasn't asked out of curiosity, rather as a question dripping with incredulity.

Friend, may I just encourage you in these moments? Choose to speak softly. Let humility and kindness guard your heart. Keep tuning your ear to the Father's voice and press on. Be patient and give people time to process the new you. If you've wounded them in the past, give them time to heal. An attempt to convince them you're different is sometimes rooted in pride anyway. Trust the Lord with the people in your past, and continue to surrender your future to Him.

Often times it may be that your changed life will eventually speak louder than any message you've been wanting to share with them anyway. God will handle the fallout of your transformation. You can trust Him with it.

Have you ever experienced resistance to your transformed life from your closest friends and family? How has Jesus helped you to overcome that?

AMBUSHED

Jesus turned to Peter and said, "Get away from me, Satan!
You are a dangerous trap to me. You are seeing things
merely from a human point of view, not from God's."
Matthew 16:23 NLT

I CAN'T TELL YOU HOW MANY times I've been prone to tell Jesus He has no clue how to handle my problems. In fact, I can be completely convinced of God's ability to do the impossible in other people's lives and still question Him on how it will be accomplished in my own. Like Peter, I can be tempted into only seeing people, problems, and situations through a human lens. While each of our struggles to trust God may vary—"I'll never be able to overcome this addiction. I'll never overcome my depression. My prodigal child will never come home"—the issue isn't in the struggle we face. The issue is in how we view our struggle.

I was struck by Jesus's words when He called Peter "Satan." Jesus went on to say that Peter was a "dangerous trap" to Him. Why? Because trapped is exactly where we will end up emotionally and spiritually if we only view life through a human lens. We will be trapped into cycles of negative thinking, depression, and hopelessness. We will be trapped into thinking God is not good or able to work in our circumstances, believing He is powerless to do anything more than what we can humanly imagine.

Interestingly, most ambushes happen after a trap has been set. It's no different with our Enemy. If we can be trapped, we can expect an ambush. So what do we do? We ask Jesus to help us see our circumstances through His eyes. We ask Him to help us filter our circumstances through the lens of His goodness, power, and justice. Our peace will only be as deep as our confidence in God's power. Jesus can give us His mindset on earthly matters, we need only to ask.

Have you ever been trapped into hopeless thinking by merely looking at your circumstances through a human lens? What do you think would happen if you asked God to give you His vision?

WHEN OUR
STRENGTH FALTERS

As they sailed across, Jesus settled down for a nap. But soon a fierce storm came down on the lake. The boat was filling with water, and they were in real danger. The disciples went and woke him up, shouting, "Master, Master, we're going to drown!" When Jesus woke up, he rebuked the wind and the raging waves. Suddenly the storm stopped and all was calm. Then he asked them, "Where is your faith?"
Luke 8:23–25 NLT

DURING ONE OF THE MOST TERRIFYING experiences on the sea for His experienced fishermen, we find Jesus napping. Unbelievable. It's not that He was dozing that has rocked me to my core. Rather, it was the question He asked His men after rebuking the very thing that terrified them that has intrigued me.

"Where is your faith?" What a question! It made sense though. Had I been there, I'm sure my faith would have been in perfect sailing weather. My faith would have been in my ability to make my way back to shore safely. I can't imagine the disciples' faith was in anything different. It was only when they were out of options to save themselves that they found themselves crying out for Jesus to rescue them.

Jesus is still asking us today, "Child, where is your faith? Are you trying to calm the waves of life yourself? Trying to get back to shore under your own strength? Do you not see that I am right here and that I am not threatened by your storm?"

We cannot afford to miss this very important message: Jesus's authority over the wind and the waves that seek to threaten our livelihoods today has not diminished since the beginning of time. Let's choose to exercise our faith not as a final resource, but as our first response.

Have you found it easier to try and fix your own problems before asking God for help? Why do you think that is? How do you think your faith would grow if you decided to call on Jesus for help first?

KNOWLEDGE AND WISDOM

The instructions of the Lord are perfect, reviving the soul.
The decrees of the Lord are trustworthy,
making wise the simple.
Psalm 19:7 NLT

IT'S REPORTED THAT "THE AVERAGE GLOBAL consumer spends 82 hours per week consuming information. Assuming an average of seven hours of sleep per night, this means that 69% of our waking hours are engaged in consuming information. For many consumers in developed markets, that number is likely closer to 100%. It's not often many people disconnect from information sources. Even when we're not in front of a screen, the nearest one is always in our pocket, or there's music or a podcast playing in the background. As a result, we consume almost 90x more information in terms of bits today than we did in 1940 and 4x more than we did less than twenty years ago."[1]

You would think access to so much information would make

[1] Doug Clinton, "Defining the Future of Human Information Consumption," June 12, 2018, *Loupventures*, https://loupventures.com/defining-the-future-of-human-information-consumption/.

us the wisest people who have ever lived. Then why is it we can act like some of the most foolish? Perhaps it is because we are spending too much time filling our minds with the things of this world that we no longer have time to fill it with the things of God.

We may never be without access to global information, so we must remember that true wisdom isn't rooted in head knowledge. True wisdom comes from a relationship with God. It comes from reading, meditating on, and working His Word into our daily lives. True wisdom comes through having a relationship with God and listening to His Spirit leading us along our way. Obtaining wisdom will never happen by accident; it is something we must pursue with our whole hearts.

So let's work to be intentional about growing in wisdom by making time for it amid the constant flow of data coming at us.

Have you ever considered knowledge and wisdom to be the same thing? Can you see the difference? What can you do today to build the wisdom of God into your life?

A LIFE-CHANGING EVENT

The man who had been freed from the demons begged to
go with him. But Jesus sent him home, saying, "No, go
back to your family, and tell them everything God has
done for you." So he went all through the town proclaim-
ing the great things Jesus had done for him.

Luke 8:38–39 NLT

HAVE YOU EVER ENCOUNTERED A PERSON who was truly possessed by a demon? I don't know that I have. But I'm encouraged as I read this story in the book of Luke, as it reminds me of God's ability to set anyone free from a demonic spirit. Even a person who is possessed by five thousand of them.

In this story Jesus arrived in a new town by boat. Upon His arrival, a wild, naked, and homeless man approached Him and asked why He was there. Jesus asked the man's name.

"Legion," he replied, for he was filled with many demons" (v. 30)

Keep in mind in that day, a Roman legion had between five to six thousand soldiers. This poor man was saying he was filled with thousands of demons. As the story goes, Jesus cast the demons out of the man and they entered into a herd of pigs that were grazing nearby. The demon-filled pigs then jumped off a cliff and died, and the man's sanity was restored.

Soon the townspeople found out about this man's deliverance and instead of rejoicing with him, they fret over the loss of their pigs. They then had the audacity to ask Jesus to leave!

As Jesus made His way back to the boat, the man who had been delivered from the demons begged to leave with Him. Jesus told him no. Instead He instructed him to return to his family and "tell them everything God had done." Was Jesus being mean? No. He was being strategic. Jesus knew this man's testimony would speak volumes to the townspeople. His story of deliverance would provide the evidence of Christ's ability to save, which was a message many in the town probably still needed to hear.

I can certainly understand this man's desire to leave and be with Jesus wherever He might go. I too have often found myself longing to be with Him more than the world I remain in. But this story serves as a good reminder that we share the same responsibility to share our stories of deliverance as this man did. We must also continue to tell others everything God has done for us.

Why do you think the townspeople responded the way they did? Has the fear of God doing something life changing in your midst ever make you wish He would leave you alone? Why?

RESTING IN THE SHADOWS

Have mercy on me, O God, have mercy! I look to you for
protection. I will hide beneath the shadow of your wings
until the danger passes by.
Psalm 57:1 NLT

GENERALLY SPEAKING, I DON'T THINK ANYONE enjoys being in the shadows. Heaven forbid we feel as if we must remain in someone else's. We run away from shadows when we see them in the oceans, not knowing what lurks underneath. Children are convinced a boogeyman is hiding under their beds. Why? Because shadows are dark, and darkness is unpredictable.

So why does King David refer to God's shadowing wings offering him a covering of protection? Perhaps he was writing this while hiding in the shadows of a cave while running from King Saul. Perhaps the cave's darkness represented to him the security God was providing him. In the face of his frustration of being hunted down, it was in this dark place David could sense the Lord's presence and recognize God's powerful protection.

Why does this matter? I think because we need to remember

that the dark and shadowy places we can find ourselves in aren't always evidence of God's absence. In fact, like the cave was for King David, it could be that the darkness we periodically find ourselves in is actually God's protection from an enemy seeking to destroy us. The shadows may be evidence of God's mercy in our lives. Perhaps we don't need to run from the shadows cast by the wings of God—rather we just need to rest there. I have found the dark is never too dark if God is with me. May it be the same for you today.

Have you ever found yourself in a dark place and wondered if God was still with you? How has God revealed His presence to you when you've entered into the shadow of His wings? What was it like when you walked out of the dark place and into the light again? Was God's presence felt in the light as it was in the dark?

RADIO SILENCE

*Call to me and I will answer you, and will tell you great
and hidden things that you have not known.*
Jeremiah 33:3 NLT

WHY DOES SHE HEAR SO CLEARLY *from God and all I get is radio silence?*
Have you ever thought that? I have. In fact, I can confess that I
have even become jealous of how others have heard from God.
Does He only speak to some of His children? Are we left only to
garner wisdom from others' God-given insights? Are we supposed
to depend on someone else's relationship with God to provide us
direction on how to live? No, I don't think so.

When Jesus said in John 10:27 that His sheep hear and follow
His voice, He is saying He has given us a direct line to Him just as
a child has to their parents. God is telling us that when we come
to Him, He will tell us great and hidden things that He desires for
us to know. The issue isn't in God's ability to communicate to His
children, because He created us to communicate with Him. The
issue is in our ability to discern His voice when He speaks to us.

So how can we begin to better understand when God is speaking? Well, it takes effort and carving out intentional time to spend in His Word. It takes time spent in worship and time just spent in silence before Him. God has already promised that He will communicate with us. Perhaps today is the day we commit to become better listeners.

Have you ever thought God only speaks to some of His children? What has your journey of learning to hear God's voice felt like in the past? Do you believe you have the tools now to better discern His voice?

CARRYING OTHERS' BURDENS WELL

Carry each other's burdens, and in this way you
will fulfill the law of Christ.
Galatians 6:2 NIV

DO YOU CARRY OTHERS' BURDENS, OR do you pick up their offenses? I've found it can be tricky sometimes to discern the difference between the two.

In Scripture it is clear we are to carry one another's burdens. Unfortunately I often see an accidental, albeit well meaning, twisting of this mandate. It's when the "burdens" we carry are actually others' offenses we pick up along life's way. Our friends come to us weighed down because someone or something has hurt them, and rather than taking it to Jesus for healing, they pick at that wound until it infects everyone around them.

Then, instead of our lovingly redirecting that person back to emotional and spiritual health, we inadvertently pick up the offense on behalf of our friend. It begins to feel as though it happened to us. We think we are helping to "carry their burden," but their offendedness becomes a weight we were never meant to bear. Soon it becomes an us-against-them situation involving people who were never involved in the conflict to begin with. I have seen multiple female friendships brought down by picking up someone else's area of woundedness. In fact, by allowing this to happen, we are granting ourselves permission to live vicariously through another person's woundedness. Moreover, because we didn't personally experience of the situation, we cannot legitimately receive healing from wounds that weren't ours to begin with. What a mess we can find ourselves in when we were just trying to help.

To effectively carry our friends' burdens, we need to pray for wisdom so we can love, lend support, and encourage others without it detrimentally impacting our own emotional and spiritual health. Our goal should always be to point people to Jesus for healing. After all, He is the one who is our ultimate and perfect burden bearer. In our attempt to love well, let's not confuse carrying others' burdens with picking up their offenses.

Have you ever thought you were picking up a burden and found yourself picking up an offense instead? How did you find freedom from it?

SERVING HIS PURPOSES

All whose hearts were stirred and whose spirits were
moved came and brought their sacred offerings to the
Lord. They brought all the materials needed for the Taber-
nacle, for the performance of its rituals, and for the sacred
garments. Both men and women came,
all whose hearts were willing.
Exodus 35:21–22 NLT

IN THE BOOK OF EXODUS, MOSES was tasked with building a tabernacle where God's manifest presence among the Israelites would reside. It was a place where the Israelite people would be able to go to worship Him. Building it would have been an extraordinary undertaking, and I wonder if Moses ever thought, *How in the world is this gonna happen?*

When God calls us to action, I think we can find ourselves questioning how everything is going to work out. Like how the finances are going to come in or whether volunteers are going to show up, not to mention battling the fear of failure that comes with every important task.

Today, God is continuing to stir our hearts and constantly making an appeal to our spirits to serve His purposes. We can tell when this stirring begins because it's as though this burning desire engulfs us and we can't find rest until we discover the place where He wants us to serve Him.

His call to us will include our using our time, our personalities, our talents, and our skill sets to accomplish His tasks. If you've been sensing God's call on your life today, I can assure you; He will provide you with opportunities you didn't even know existed! And just a note of encouragement: We don't need to have all the answers about how it will all work out before we begin the work. We are simply to surrender to the Lord and trust Him to accomplish His purposes through our obedience.

Have you ever taken inventory of how you have been created and how that can serve the purposes of God? What can you do today to begin to participate in God's plans and purposes for your life?

STEADFAST LOVE

May the Lord direct your hearts to the love of God
and to the steadfastness of Christ.
2 Thessalonians 3:5 ESV

WE LIVE IN A WORLD WHERE love feels like it needs to be earned, that we must perform in such a way to keep the love that has been dangled in front of us. It doesn't take long, however, to discover that love can be lost. Your spouse may betray you. Friends may desert you. An employer may fire you. Your family may reject you. And you're left feeling unlovable and wondering if being loved was ever something that could be depended on.

I think that's one of the main reasons God's "steadfast love" toward us is mentioned 196 times in the Old Testament and 127 times in the Psalms alone. God does not want us to confuse man's love with His love. His steadfast love for us is unchanging, immovable, and firmly fixed upon us. We don't have to perform to get it, and we don't have to fail to lose it.

Friend, the Lord is going out of His way to remind you that He is always looking upon you through the eyes of love. In practical terms, He remembers your birthday and knows your favorite color. He knows when you wake up in the morning and when you go to bed at night. He knows every secret you keep and every sorrow you hide. He knows what will get you excited and where you feel let down. He walks with you during the day and watches over you at night. He doesn't require perfect behavior, perfect attendance, or perfect prayers. It's time we stop striving to earn God's love and just live in it.

If you are feeling less than loved today by those around you, look to Jesus. Ask Him to give you the ability to grasp how deep His love is for you. You'll find it's real. It's powerful. And it's steadfast.

Have you ever felt like you needed to be perfect for God to love you? Does the word *steadfast* change your understanding of God's love? How does it make you feel knowing He loves you apart from your performance?

GIFTINGS AND JEALOUSY

*But Moses replied, "Are you jealous for my sake? I wish
that all the Lord's people were prophets and that the Lord
would put His Spirit upon them all!"*
Numbers 11:29 NLT

HAVE YOU EVER BECOME JEALOUS OF the giftings God has given other people? Why do we seem to struggle with resentment when we should be celebrating what the Lord is doing through their lives? Maybe we are tempted to think that what they are doing is something we wish we were doing. This results in our joy being stolen from doing the tasks the Lord has placed in front of us. We view our work as less than from what God has given another to do.

We don't mean for that to happen, of course, but it does. I'm grateful Moses provides us with a great response when those emotions rise up. Numbers 11:26–29 reads, "Two men, Eldad and Medad, had stayed behind in the camp. They were listed among the elders, but they had not gone out to the tabernacle. Yet the Spirit rested upon them as well, so they prophesied there in the camp. A young man ran and reported to Moses, 'Eldad and Medad are prophesying in the camp!' Joshua son of Nun, who had been Moses' assistant since his youth, protested, 'Moses, my master, make them stop!' But Moses replied, 'Are you jealous for my sake? I wish that all the Lord's people were prophets and that the Lord would put His Spirit upon them all!'"

What a mark of confidence in God and in His calling. Moses wanted God's Spirit to fall on all people, regardless if they were with him or not. This means that operating in our giftings and watching others operate in theirs should always be void of jealousy. The Lord will lead you into all of the plans and purposes He has for you, just as He will lead others. So let's resist envying others and choose instead to cheer them on! May it be our deepest desire that the Lord's Spirit fall on all people.

Have you ever been jealous of the gifts God has given other people? What has God shown you about your own giftings? How can you celebrate what God is doing through others around you without envy?

JESUS, TAKE 'EM DOWN!

He loved to curse others; now you curse him.
He never blessed others; now don't you bless him.
Psalm 109:17 NLT

KING DAVID KNEW HOW TO POUR out his frustration to the Lord! The entirety of Psalm 109 reveals his brokenness over feeling rejected, hated, and falsely accused. In this passage, David was essentially tattling on those who had hurt him as he told God, "Look how bad this person is; now deal with him accordingly!" In all honesty, I'm grateful for David's words here because it invites us to pour out our broken hearts before God without shame.

Like David, I've attempted to call down God's wrath on people who have caused me grief. I've tried to persuade the Lord that they were His enemies as well. I mean, if they had offended me, then certainly they had offended Him. "Take 'em down, Jesus!" would be the best description of my prayers.

That said, I've discovered that God doesn't always respond to our enemies in the way we want Him to. Instead, God is marked by His slowness to anger, His unfailing love, and His forgiveness of every kind of sin and rebellion. Oh sure, we can ask that God deliver a harsh response to those who have hurt us, but we shouldn't be surprised if He brings about redemption instead.

So let's leave our broken pieces with the Lord. We can be honest like King David and tell God the best way we think He should respond. But when we've finished, when we've said all the words, let's leave room for God to respond however He'd like to. You can trust He will do the right way and at the right time. He knows how you feel. He knows the pain. He can be trusted to handle every bit of it.

Have you ever told God exactly how to handle your enemies? Have you ever experienced His response in a different manner than what you envisioned? What have you learned through that?

IDOLATRY

Why let the nations say, "Where is their God?" Our God is in the heavens, and he does as he wishes. Their idols are merely things of silver and gold, shaped by human hands. They have mouths but cannot speak, and eyes but cannot see. They have ears but cannot hear, and noses but cannot smell. They have hands but cannot feel, and feet but cannot walk, and throats but cannot make a sound. And those who make idols are just like them, as all who trust in them.

Psalm 115:2–8 NLT

HAVE YOU EVER FELT JUST COMPLETELY spiritually ineffective? Looked around at others and wondered why they seem to have this vibrant walk with God that you seem to be missing? Questioned why you've never sensed God's presence as they have? Then perhaps it is time to take inventory of where, or rather in what, you have placed your trust.

A quick inventory of our lives will reveal if we have fallen prey to trusting in our paychecks, 401(k)s, degrees, bigger homes, nicer cars, social standings, or other things to propel us forward in life. Perhaps we have looked to them to protect us or provide for us. If this has happened, Scripture tell us we will be rendered ineffective because in God's eyes, we are practicing idolatry. And idolatry silences the powerful acts of God.

Idolatry blinds us from seeing the hand of God.

Idolatry deafens us from hearing the voice of God.

Idolatry isolates us so that we aren't able to feel the presence of God.

Idolatry silences us so that we aren't able to testify to the greatness of God.

Why? Because we are no longer trusting in God. If we want to experience the reality of God, we need to ensure our trust is in Him alone. If we do not want to become like the idols we can so easily create, we need to ensure that we have given God His rightful place on the throne of our lives and that nothing else has taken His place.

When was the last time you took inventory of where you placed your faith? Why do you find it easier to trust in what you can see versus who you can't see? What would it look like for you to trust the Lord in your situation?

IMPERFECTLY USEFUL

One day the girl said to her mistress, "I wish my master
would go to see the prophet in Samaria.
He would heal him of his leprosy."
2 Kings 5:3 NLT

"THE GIRL." JUST SOME NAMELESS GIRL. Though we don't know much
about her, we do know about her heart. It remained soft in an
impossibly hard situation. This young tenderhearted girl had been
kidnapped from Israel during a battle. As it would be, she ended
up being enslaved to a powerful warrior named Naaman, serving
as his wife's mistress. I wonder if she assumed this would just be
her lot in life. I wonder how she felt working in this home after
being kidnapped. Did she battle some depression and fear? Did she
miss her family of origin or the land where she could practice her
faith so freely? I think these are viable options, but I have found it
incredibly inspiring by what she chose to do in spite of her unimag-
inable circumstances.

While still held captive, our precious, nameless servant girl
chose to point her leprous owner to a prophet back home who

could set him free. She pointed him back to someone who could bring him hope, someone who could restore his health.

Why does this inspire me so deeply? I think it's because today we are the nameless pointers. We are now the ones who point to the One who can set others free. Like the servant girl in our passage, it doesn't matter if our circumstances feel less than ideal—we are still responsible to point others to the One who can heal them. Why? Because we know if He did it for us, He can do it for them.

Interestingly, Naaman listened to this young girl, went to see the prophet in Samaria and was healed. Through this he also discovered the One True God and ended up worshiping Him. If we want to be like any heroes of the faith we read about in Scripture, let's be like this nameless servant girl and strive to point others to the One who still brings about healing today.

Have you ever felt like your circumstances needed to be perfect to point others to Christ? Perfectly healed, perfectly positioned, perfectly educated to be useful? How has this story challenged those beliefs?

FREEDOM OVER STRONGHOLDS

For when a strong man is fully armed and guards his palace, his possessions are safe—until someone even stronger attacks and overpowers him, strips him of his weapons, and carries off his belongings.
Luke 11:21–22 NLT

STRONGHOLDS. WE ALL HAVE EXPERIENCED THEM as the hurts, hang-ups, and habits in our lives work to distract us from the good things God has for us. We give them power over us, and they quickly become the things we don't talk about. They are the things we do in secret. In fact, when strongholds have taken up residence in our lives we'll know, because we will find ourselves strategically guarding them. Hiding them. Trying to ignore them. We know it's a stronghold when it's working to set itself against the power and knowledge of God in our lives. It's idolatrous in nature and demonic in origin.

We can be deceived into thinking we will never overcome the

strongholds that are trying to control our lives and tempted to think we will never be free of the unquestionably strong things that work to keep us bound. That is why this passage in Luke is so important. The writer wants us to know a very important thing. He wants us to know that the One who can bring us freedom is *stronger* than the one who wants to keep us bound.

Satan likes to pretend he is still fully armed and certainly makes valiant attempts to safeguard the strongholds in our lives. I imagine sometimes he even entertains the idea that his possessions are safe, but thankfully, he's wrong. God sent Someone even stronger to attack and overpower him at the cross, and because of that, Satan has been stripped of his weapons! Today Jesus lives to continually, constantly, and regularly carry away Satan's belongings.

Friends, we cannot be confused about this very important matter. Satan's strength is not equal to Jesus's strength. Satan's strength is *inferior* 100 percent of the time. Jesus is our someone stronger. Don't believe for one moment that whatever stronghold that has kept you bound will keep you bound forever. Instead, call on Jesus to set you free. You will discover He is strong enough to do it.

Can you identify what you would call a stronghold in your life? Do you believe Jesus is strong enough to set you free? What would it look like you to walk in freedom from that today?

IN THE MIDDLE OF THE NIGHT

Rise during the night and cry out. Pour out your hearts like water to the Lord. Lift up your hands to him in prayer, pleading for your children, for in every street they are faint with hunger.
Lamentations 2:19 NLT

THE MAJORITY OF WHAT PARENTS SHARE on social media about their kids has everything to do with their successes and nothing to do with their failures. I don't think our kids would necessarily enjoy their struggles being posted for the whole world to see. Neither would any good parent, unless they honestly thought that sharing it might help someone else. However, this got me thinking about the things we are required to keep private but deep down would really like someone to know. Maybe to just simply feel like someone else really understands our pain.

Perhaps you are in a "middle of the night" situation with your child who is "hungry" for the things of this world and is currently feasting on things you know will only bring them sorrow. Maybe they have stopped listening to you and have blocked out the voices of other wise counselors who have surrounded them.

I think this is why the passage found in Lamentations means so much to me. Jesus is not a friend who tires of our calls, our messages, our weariness, or our pain. He is aware of what is happening with our children, and He is the only One who really cares enough to deliver them from what is keeping them bound.

Friends, this verse tells me that the Lord desires that we pour out our hearts like water to Him. It tells me that we should continually be lifting up our hands in prayer and pleading for our children. Our perfect heavenly Father is listening, present, and willing to hear from us. He stands poised, ready to respond, restore, and redeem every broken situation. Truly He is our confident hope and sure help for all these matters concerning our children.

Have you ever come to the place where you recognized your need for God's help in raising your kids? What would it look like for you to plead for your children before God?

CONFIDENT ATTACK

And a voice from heaven said, "This is my Son,
whom I love; with him I am well pleased."
Matthew 3:17 NIV

ALTHOUGH WE CAN STRUGGLE TO FIND confidence, it didn't evade Jesus. In fact, He lived fully confident of three things revealed in this verse: He was secure in His identity as the Son of God. He was loved and therefore had a strong sense of belonging. He knew His approval wasn't based on His performance. Because we are God's children, we can also be assured of His approval of us in these areas as well.

We shouldn't be surprised then that Satan works hard to attack us in all three of those areas.

When attacking our sense of *identity*, Satan says, "Look inward to discover yourself." But God says, "Look upward and discover Me. Real living can't be found apart from Me because I have plans for your life that far exceed anything you could dream for yourself."

When attacking our sense of *belonging*, Satan says, "You don't belong anywhere; you don't fit in. No one likes you." But God says,

"You're a part of my family now. I have grafted you in. Adopted you as my own. You are now My child in whom I greatly delight!"

When attacking our sense of *acceptance*, Satan says, "You are such a failure. A sinner. You never do anything right. God will definitely stop loving you now. You're such a reject." But God says, "My grace is a gift to you. You can't earn it. Nothing you do will cause Me to love you any more or any less. I love you because I am love."

It's time for us to walk in confidence in these three areas as well. Why? Because knowing who we are in Christ solidifies our sense of belonging, and the fact that we have been accepted by God enables us to live the life He has for us. Knowing who we are in Christ has the power to change everything.

Have you ever felt Satan attack those three areas in your life? What steps have you taken or will you take to combat it?

FAITHFUL COMPANIONS

I will search for faithful people to be my companions.
Only those who are above reproach will be allowed
to minister to me.
Psalm 101:6 NLT

WHY DOES NAVIGATING FEMALE FRIENDSHIPS FEEL so complicated? Is it because of past betrayals? Do we feel insecure when deepening our level of intimacy with others, thinking, *If they knew me, they wouldn't like me?* Do we struggle with not feeling good enough to fit in around certain groups of women? Perhaps you have other reasons, but as I tell my daughter, cultivating wise female friendships is important because they don't just happen.

Thankfully God's Word gives us guidelines that provide wisdom in discerning whom we grant heart access to. It helps us to know what to watch for and what to take into consideration when making wise choices in friendship.

In practical terms of being a good friend, how do we "walk with the wise and become wise" and not "associate with fools and get in trouble" (Prov. 13:20)? We can look for women who are actively serving the Lord, as well women who are actively seeking to honor God in their marriages, work, parenting, and other friendships. We would also be wise in allowing enough time to pass before we begin expressing loyal alignments to anyone. Time is a beautiful thing in the friendship greenhouse.

We want to look for women who speak life-giving words to others around them. You'll know this if they point you to Jesus in the middle of the mess. Look for girlfriends who will speak life over you, which is vital, as the world seeks to suffocate it right out of you. Serving as mutual sources of encouragement has the ability to carry friendships over many years.

You won't find a perfect friend because no one is perfect, but the Lord through His Word helps facilitate life-giving friendships. Also, while you are looking for godly friendships, work on becoming a godly friend. Ask the Lord to bring the women who you're meant to invest in and who are meant to invest in you. Don't ever forget that you're worth knowing and being loved well. Life-sustaining friendships are always worth doing God's way.

Have you ever rushed into a friendship and found yourself in a place of bondage rather than freedom? How do you think that could have been avoided? Do you think God has friends in store for your life and you're willing to trust Him to provide?

FAITH IN ACTION

And he said to her, "Daughter, your faith has
made you well. Go in peace. Your suffering is over."
Mark 5:34 NLT

FAITH ISN'T PASSIVE, SENDING SOMEONE GOOD thoughts, well wishes, or light and love. Rather, faith engages every part of who we are and requires us to act upon our belief in God and His Word, which results in our experiencing inexplicable things from Him. Faith is living in such a way where we have these powerful encounters with a living God who changes everything about and around us.

Mark 5:25–34 tells us of the faith of a woman who had been suffering for twelve years with constant bleeding. In her day, this infirmity resulted in her being both a social and religious outcast. She couldn't be touched without those touching her becoming ceremonially unclean. For this woman, it had been a very long time since she had felt anyone's loving arms wrapped around her or been allowed to attend any of the religious gatherings or festivals her community was built upon. After spending all her money on the best doctors and not receiving any sort of a cure, she was probably feeling isolated and desperate. So she bled on, continuing to live a life of scorn and rejection—until Jesus came on the scene.

When this woman heard about Jesus, her faith activated every fiber of her being. As we read in an earlier devotion, she traveled to Him and reached out to touch Him and ended up talking with Him. Jesus responded to her great faith and healed her. In that moment she felt His healing power flow through her. Her suffering ended and Jesus sent her away in peace. What a tender and beautiful gift of new life for this woman.

I think she is very much like us. How often do we put our faith in every other alternative to God to fix our moral, financial, relational, emotional, and physical illnesses? We can chase down every other answer we think is available to us, all the while ignoring the fact that our ultimate healing can only come from Jesus alone. The beauty wasn't simply that Jesus healed her body but that He healed her mind and spirit too. Years of pain, fear, isolation, and frustration replaced with ultimate healing and powerful peace. Our God is good. Our faith in Him is sure. Only God knows what He has planned for us, so like our woman in this story, let's put a little action to our faith in what He has for us.

Do you feel your behavior reflects your faith in God? Have you ever experienced His healing and power in your everyday life? What was that like for you?

WHEN FANTASY SPEAKS

This is all the more urgent, for you know how late it is;
time is running out. Wake up, for our salvation is nearer
now than when we first believed.
Romans 13:11 NLT

I AM SHOCKED AT HOW MUCH time I've wasted on mindless things that don't really matter. I hate that because I don't want to waste any moment of my life. If we really want to live a life of purpose, we need to take inventory of how we are spending our time as there are so many things that fill our daily agendas that we don't plan for.

For instance, is our free time consumed with TV shows that shape unrealistic goals for our lives? Do they tempt us to believe we would be better off if we just lived in a house like that? Were married to a man like that? Had money like her? Were as smart as him? Could decorate a house like her? Cooked like him? Could fit in that size again? Friend, if we are spending the majority of our time wishing we were created as someone else, living someplace else, we will miss what God has created us for.

If we want our lives to matter for the Lord, then we need to stop focusing on the things that this world thinks are important and shift our focus to what God says is important. We can do this by choosing to surround ourselves with friends who will encourage us with godly counsel. We can work to take our thoughts captive and make them obedient to Christ. We can remove the lies we've believed for so many years and replace them with the truth of God's Word. We can exchange the fear and anxiety that comes with being consumed with the things of this world for the peace that God gives us when we are consumed with Him.

Jesus is coming again soon, friend—that is a fact. What is it that God desires to accomplish through our lives before that day comes? I don't know. But I do know that we will only find it by carving out time to sit in God's presence and hearing from Him. Maybe it's time to take inventory, silence the noise, and ask the Lord how we can best use our time to fulfill His plans and purposes for us, instead of wasting our lives pursuing the world's agenda over His.

Have you taken inventory of your time recently? Were you able to find areas that could be realigned to make room for more important things? Did you find more purpose in your life?

THE SECRET KEEPERS

God revealed their secret to Peter.
Acts 5:3 TPT

HAVE YOU EVER DISCOVERED A SECRET that a child, spouse, or friend has been keeping from you? Maybe you read a text message you weren't meant to see, found a letter from a lover that had been tucked away, or happened upon a social media account you never knew existed. It's nearly impossible to describe the sickening feeling in your stomach as you remember those first painful moments of discovery.

In Acts, we discover a secret that Ananias and Sapphira had kept from the apostle Peter. This husband and wife team had sold some property to raise money for ministry, but they secretly withheld some of the proceeds and told Peter they were bringing the full amount as a donation to the apostles. Personally, I'm sad that they even felt like they had to lie. In biblical times, giving was an act of the heart—it wasn't a requirement.

As God would have it, He revealed their secret to Peter, and the rest of the story has a tragic ending that reveals just how seriously

God views our honesty. Friend, today God doesn't reveal secrets in order to bring condemnation but in order to convict and bring about healing. This means we can trust Him with secrets (both ours and others) because He can be depended on to handle what we know and what we do not.

It's a terrible thing to feel like someone is lying to us, but we can stop trying to "catch" people lying because God knows everything. John 16:13 says the Holy Spirit will lead us into all truth. You can ask Him to reveal any hidden things, and He will let you know if, and when, the time is right for us to know. Moreover, He will give us the wisdom to handle whatever must come next. There is great peace in knowing that you can trust the Lord with everything you know as well as everything you don't.

Do you remember the last time you discovered someone was lying to you? How did it make you feel? How does it make you feel knowing that God sees everything and when the time is right, can reveal whatever you need to know? Do you feel like you can trust Him to handle the things you do not know?

LOVE RIGHT WHERE YOU ARE

*The Son of Man, on the other hand, feasts and drinks,
and you say, "He's a glutton and a drunkard, and a friend
of tax collectors and other sinners!"
But wisdom is shown to be right by its results.*
Matthew 1:19 NLT

I'M OFTEN CHALLENGED THAT JESUS SPENT so much time with sinners He was often accused of being one. He shared His meals with them (Luke 19:1–10), healed them (Mark 2:17), and ultimately died for them (Rom. 5:8).

I think it challenges me because it defies my understanding of what it means to be holy and set apart. Christ didn't ostracize those who weren't like Him. Instead, He lived among them and loved them well.

I wonder if it might be time for us to question if we are engaging the world immediately around us just as Jesus did, without the fear that we will somehow lose our "holiness" in the process. The real question is: Am I loving in such a way that I could be accused of being a sinner by those who consider themselves the most righteous?

Honestly, I wonder if that's the true litmus test for how well we are loving those around us. God never worried about Jesus's reputation when He spent time with sinners but wanted His Son to show His love to all people. God's goal hasn't changed, and it remains that we continue to show His love to a lost and hurting world. If we're going to be accused of anything, let's decide to be okay with being accused of loving as Jesus did.

How will you let the love of Jesus help you love others well?

OUR PAST SINS

*Then Judas threw the silver coins down in the Temple and
went out and hanged himself.*
Matthew 27:5 NLT

IT'S INTERESTING THAT BOTH PETER AND Judas betrayed Jesus. The difference between them is that Peter repented, and Judas hung himself.

I wonder if a little internal analysis would reveal that we are all a little more like Judas than we would like to think. We may not hang ourselves with a rope, but we hang ourselves in ways we never thought we would.

Rather than allowing ourselves to receive the tender and forgiving words of Jesus for the sins we've committed that day, we hang ourselves on the rope of self-condemnation. I mean, how many of us have resorted to cutting and self-harming rather than allowing the blood that Jesus already shed to cover our sins, restore us, and bring us peace? How often have we misused prescription medication to escape the pain of our past or the shame of our guilt? How have we inadvertently stifled the growth of our spiritual life by not attending church because we feel too guilty to walk in? How many of us have stopped reading our Bibles because we're convinced God won't speak to us again since we didn't listen last time?

In almost twenty years of doing women's ministry, I have discovered that we will do whatever we think necessary to make ourselves pay for our sins against God, or at minimum try and distance ourselves from Him because of our shame.

Friend, it's time we stop getting "hung up" on our "hang-ups." We may have acted like Judas, but we can be forgiven like Peter. Jesus longs to restore us to right standing. He sits waiting for our arrival and our repentant heart. We simply need to take one step toward Him and He will run to meet us. Nothing delights God more than seeing us return to Him. He makes it known that there is no condemnation in His face as He turns toward us offering His forgiveness, love, and a fresh start. He did with Peter. He did it for me. Let Him do it for you!

Have you ever tried to "hang" yourself to make yourself pay for your past sins? How has that worked out for you? What would it look like for you to really allow yourself to receive Christ's forgiveness?

MOVING AWAY

The LORD keeps watch over you as you come and go,
both now and forever.
Psalm 121:8 NLT

DURING A RECENT SUMMER VACATION, MY youngest son jumped in the ocean with his newly purchased boogie board and, with no thought to his safety, he began playing in the small waves that were coming up to the shoreline. Unfortunately, he wasn't aware that the waves were carrying him down the shoreline from where I was sitting. He became oblivious to his slow drift, and every time he rode his board in on the beach, he would stand up and look at me for approval. If I didn't appear to be where he thought I should be, he would stomp his foot in the wet sand and accuse me of moving.

Had I moved? Nope, not at all. Had I stopped watching him? No way. Clearly the ocean was far too dangerous for me to leave my child unguarded. Rather, his fun activity had moved him away from me. I've considered how similar this is to how God is with us. Often, we become so consumed with all our earthly activities that when we stand up and look toward our Heavenly Father, we can't find Him. Who moved? Well, it wasn't Him.

I have found great peace in knowing just as it is with my son playing in the ocean, no matter how far away we drift, God's never letting His eyes off us either. Interestingly, do you know where my son was most comfortable playing? Right in front of me. In fact, when he discovered he was drifting away, he would work to re-center himself in front of me. He knew the safest place to experience both danger and fun was right in front of the one who could rescue him if he needed it. I think that's where we should choose to stay with God: right in front of Him, knowing that if we begin to drift, He will be there to bring us back to the place of safety.

Have you ever felt that God has moved away from you or that you could no longer see Him? What steps do you need to take to ensure you no longer drift away from your place of safety?

WHEN IT'S HARD
TO RECONCILE

Your laws are always right;
help me to understand them so I may live.
Psalm 199:144 NLT

DO YOU DREAM OF ONE DAY becoming a great theologian? I don't. I'm pretty much just a girl who loves God, is committed to Jesus, and is mesmerized by the Holy Spirit. His written Word is my sanity and the anchor in my storms. But the more I study, I have found there are some things I have a harder time understanding in full.

I wonder if it's because some Scriptures can appear on the surface to contradict each other. Maybe it's because we read about things like slavery and concubines, plagues and laws, and we are left wondering what we are supposed to do with that? So do we respond as many do by walking away from the faith, claiming the Bible is filled with contradictions and uncomfortable truths? Do we harden our hearts and claim it's too hard to understand? Or do we settle on understanding that we don't have to fit everything together nice and neat to deeply love the God who is revealed through it? Maybe it's okay to allow the tension to exist without feeling the need to understand everything for it to be believable. Perhaps we decide to get excited that there is still more of God to discover.

For all the things I don't know and things I can't seem to reconcile, this is what I do know: God's ways are so much higher than ours; His thoughts toward us are so much more expansive than ours; His love is more intoxicating and His forgiveness so much more overflowing. Let's choose to rest in that whatever God does want us to fully understand. He will make possible for us by His Spirit.

Friends, let's not quit pursuing our faith in Jesus just because everything doesn't make sense at first, second, or even third glance. Instead, let's purpose to keep going and to trust His Spirit to show us the way. Surely there is no greater adventure than the pursuit of God and seeking to understanding His heart in all matters.

Do you know anyone who has walked away from the faith because they were unable to reconcile different aspects of it? How can you counsel them to return and trust God with what they feel they don't understand? Do you feel as though you can continue to trust God with the things you cannot understand in Scripture?

THE PERFECT MESSENGERS

You must not murder.
Exodus 20:14 NLT

AREN'T YOU GRATEFUL TO KNOW THAT God does not disqualify us from serving Him in the present based on our pasts. It's so interesting to me that God entrusted the command of "You must not murder" to a man who had done that very thing. Moses had already committed that vile act forty years earlier when he lived in Egypt. Now God was calling him to lead the Israelites into the promised land and giving him the commandments they should abide by. I wonder if Moses was inclined to think that maybe he should have been disqualified because of his past sin.

You see, that's the amazing thing about the Lord and His redemptive plan for humanity. When we have accepted Jesus's payment for our sin, He makes us messengers of His grace. He entrusts us with His commands (even the ones we've broken in our pasts) and tells us to share with others what He can do for them. We cannot continue to allow ourselves to think that our past disqualifies us from what God wants to do through us in the present. Instead we must share the good news and trust the Lord to continue His transforming work in us and in others.

If God were looking for perfect, sinless messengers, none of us would make the cut. We'd all be disqualified. When Jesus saves us, our pasts are placed squarely in the palm of God's hand, and only He determines what to do with them. For many, this serves as a living testimony that the amazing transformation He has accomplished in our lives He can do for others. So surrender your past to the Lord. Let His forgiveness flood over it, then let Him use it to build His kingdom. Perhaps God has handpicked you to be the next modern-day Moses to lead others still held captive toward freedom in Christ.

Have you ever believed you were disqualified from Christian service because of your past? How would your life change if you knew God could use even the worst circumstances to bring glory to Him?

BEING STILL IN THE CHAOS

Be still, and know that I am God!
Psalm 46:10 NLT

IF THERE WAS EVER A TIME we needed to focus on being still, it would be now. We are consumed with busyness and living insanely chaotic lives. We're working full and/or part time, raising kids, trying to maintain a healthy marriage, serving in ministries, buying groceries, preparing three healthy meals a day, and attending weddings and graduations. Maybe we're leading or attending weekly Bible studies, in counseling trying to overcome an addiction, or spending time in a hospital. Maybe we're in the middle of caring for our aging parents or wondering if we have enough money to cover the rest of the month, and somehow in the middle of all of this crazy, we're trying to figure out how to carve time into our schedules just to be still.

Is achieving stillness even possible? Interestingly, this particular "be still" is found right smack in the middle of Psalm 46:9–11. In context, it was a command from God that meant to "sink, relax, and become helpless" during a time of war. Stillness was an invitation to allow Him to take over and bring about victory within battle. It was a call for the people of Israel to acknowledge that God was both in charge of their defense and their protection.

This is important to know because when the ancients would go to war, they would fight in the name of their gods. If they won the battle, their god got all the glory. In Psalm 46:10, the Lord is essentially saying, "Relax. The victory in this battle is not dependent on you. It's on Me. You just need to relax your hold on this and become wholly dependent on Me for your success. The victory will be Mine."

We must choose to be still. In the chaos. In the busy. In the battles we face every day. It's vital because it will reveal in whom we are really trusting to bring about the victories we are so anxiously trying to achieve. So rest. Be still. Victory is on its way. God's has this. He has you.

Why do you find it so hard to be still? How do you think your life would be impacted if you chose to carve time to be still?

MINDSET OVER PERFECTION

Then he asked them, "But who do you say I am?" Simon Peter answered, "You are the Messiah, the Son of the living God." Jesus replied, "You are blessed, Simon son of John, because my Father in heaven has revealed this to you. You did not learn this from any human being."
Matthew 16:15–17 NLT

HAVE YOU EVER FELT LIKE SOMEONE'S receiving or not receiving Christ is based entirely on how well you presented the gospel to them? I'm afraid I can fall into this mindset quicker than any other.

You see, I'm a speaker by trade. A seasoned communicator. I've attended classes, training sessions, conferences, and more to learn how to deliver a biblical message effectively. I work hard at it because my greatest desire is for people to know and love Jesus as much as is humanly possible. So I put a lot of effort into crafting a message that can be understandable. But before any of that, I pray long and hard over the audiences I'll speak to and over the platforms I'll stand on. I pray over the attendees' families and anything else the Lord brings to mind so whatever is shared would fall on prepared hearts.

The problem is, if I'm not being led by the Spirit in all these matters, I can begin to feel like whether or not a message is received well is based entirely on how well I presented it or how well I prepared for it. It's tragic how quickly a message all about God quickly becomes all about me.

I think that's why this passage is so important. It reminds us all that while preparation is always good and right, we don't need to be faultless when we share the gospel with others. Our perfectly crafted messages don't hold the power to save anyone. Rather, it is the Holy Spirit's responsibility to pierce the human heart with the words that are being spoken. We must never forget that it is God who is the holder and revealer of truth. He is the one who brings about conviction and conversion. True heart change is never a result of a flawless delivery of an impeccable message. It is only accomplished by a perfect God, accomplishing His perfect will, through imperfect beings.

Have you spent time trying to be perfect so you can win others to salvation? How does it make you feel to think that only God can reveal to man their need for forgiveness and salvation? Does knowing this change the way you speak to and pray for your lost friends and family?

ALL THINGS TO ALL PEOPLE

*For we are God's masterpiece. He has created us anew in
Christ Jesus, so we can do the good things
he planned for us long ago.*
Ephesians 2:10 NLT

I LOVE TO DREAM ABOUT THE good things God has planned for each of us to accomplish in our lives. Unfortunately, sometimes it's more obvious to me to see the good things other people are doing. But rather than that serving to inspire me, watching them tends to trip me up. I have found that when I keep looking at them, I begin worrying that I should be doing whatever everyone else is doing.

For instance, I used to worry that if I didn't homeschool, I wouldn't be considered a good mom. I worried that because I didn't know how to cook, garden, or sew, I wasn't a good wife. Did I need the entire Bible memorized to be considered a good Bible teacher? Did I have to personally carry everyone's burdens to be considered a good friend? It soon became evident that I had fallen prey to wanting to do all the good things I was watching others do around me. I was consumed with worry that I should be living *their* lives and was completely missing what God had for mine.

Friend, we cannot do every good thing that everyone else is doing and accomplish the good things God has planned for *our* lives. Well-intentioned people will inadvertently put pressure on you to fulfill what they think are the best plans for your life because they have found them good for *their* lives. But what God has planted in each one of us might look different from what He has planted in your friends. We need wisdom to know exactly what we should say yes to and what we need to say no to. Thankfully this is the kind of wisdom the Lord provides to us. God's good plans for you may look completely different than what your friends are doing. In fact, it may look vastly different that anything you've even *experienced* thus far. So today, let's stop looking *around* at what everyone else is doing and start looking *up* for what God planned for us from a long time ago!

Have you ever felt like you needed to be doing more than what God has you doing? How have you discovered God's good plans for your life so far? Have they differed from what you thought they were? Does it make you feel as though there are more ahead?

UNLIKELY GREATNESS

*Later, Joseph of Arimathea asked Pilate for the body of Je-
sus. Now Joseph was a disciple of Jesus, but secretly because
he feared the Jewish leaders. With Pilate's permission,
he came and took the body away. He was accompanied
by Nicodemus, the man who earlier had visited Jesus at
night. Nicodemus brought a mixture of myrrh and aloes,
about seventy-five pounds. Taking Jesus' body, the two of
them wrapped it, with the spices, in strips of linen. This
was in accordance with Jewish burial customs.*

John 19:38–40 NIV

IT WASN'T HIS DISCIPLES WHO BROUGHT Jesus down and carefully wrapped
His lifeless body in strips of linen. It wasn't His circle of followers who brought expensive fragrances to anoint His body before
it's burial. It wasn't the people who had received a miracle by His
touch who gently wrapped His pierced hands. It wasn't His most
vocal supporters who positioned His body just right on the stone
platform inside the tomb.

No, in fact most all of those who claimed to love Jesus had fled
the scene.

Instead, it was two secret followers of Jesus who garnered the courage to do what needed to be done. Two men who had previously been afraid to admit Jesus was who He said He was were the ones who decided to publicly carry the greatest weight that had ever been carried. The weight of hopes dashed and the weight of sorrow magnified. The weight of the desecrated body of the Savior of the world.

What does this tell me? This tells me that those with the loudest voices, the biggest platforms, or the greatest circle of social influence do not necessarily hold the monopoly on the most important jobs. Though these men, Joseph and Nicodemus, may have preferred the background rather than center stage, I think God smiled down on them that day as they cared for the body of Jesus. How precious that service must have been to His heart. I don't think these two formerly silent followers were ever the same. I don't think they all of a sudden became limelight seekers, but I think they learned that even background people are given some of the greatest responsibilities.

If you tend to be on the more private side, don't downplay your personality or see it as a negative when it comes to your serving God within your day and time. Your life as a child of God still has a starring role in His story.

Have you ever felt like you needed to be more vocal or more influential to be used by God? How does it make you feel that you simply need to be obedient to be used greatly by God?

SELECTIVE HEARING

For God speaks again and again,
though people do not recognize it.
Job 33:14 NLT

OUR DAUGHTER WAS BORN HEARING IMPAIRED. The actual clinical diagnosis was given to us when she was three. While not entirely deaf, she has what is called a "genetically related, moderate-to-severe hearing loss" in both ears. She wears hearing aids, and when they are working properly, she can hear better than those without any sort of hearing loss.

I asked her a question once. "Morgan, have you ever asked God to heal your ears?" to which she replied, "No, why would I? I can tune people out when I'm tired of listening to them!" After giggling at her response, I began to think about her answer a bit deeper. You see, she struggles to hear anything when she first gets up in the morning. The silence afforded to her during the sleeping hours will dull her ability to hear even a little bit. In fact, when she wakes up it will take her some time to adjust to the sounds around her before she puts her hearing aids in. Interestingly, she is skilled at reading lips and if she is watching you speak, she can generally make out what you're saying without her hearing aids. For her to do that requires her to focus closely on your face. If she works to tune out all the noises around her, she can "hear" you. Not like how you and I hear, but how she can.

Then it hit me—all of us are born with a hearing deficiency. The world continually screams for our attention, and sin deafens us to the voice of the Lord. Often God chooses not to compete with the noise of the world. He doesn't have to. His voice is soft, calming. It is up to us to tune out all the other voices, turn our faces to His, and focus on His voice. We must get quiet enough to listen. Just like my daughter can hear you unaided based on her proximity to you, we too can hear God based on our proximity to Him. Friend, when you turn toward Him, looking intently at His face and intentionally tune out the other voices, His voice will become louder. What you couldn't hear before will suddenly become so clear.

Have you found it hard to hear from God? Is there anything in your life that may need to be turned down or tuned out so you can better tune in?

HITTING ROCK BOTTOM

When they heard that the Lord was concerned about them
and had seen their misery,
they bowed down and worshiped.
Exodus 4:31 NLT

IMAGINE YOU HAVE JUST BEEN TOLD that the Lord had seen your suffering and was coming to deliver you. Only instead of things getting better, they immediately get worse. Instead of being on a spiritual high, you're barely surviving at the bottom of the spiritual pit. You trusted God. You worshiped thinking your freedom was coming. But now the only emotion you feel is that God has failed you.

I think the Israelites knew exactly how that must have felt. They had been enslaved for over four hundred years and had just been told their freedom was coming. But what happened next? More beatings and higher quotas to meet by their slave masters.

Perhaps Moses and Aaron had the same thoughts as the Israelites did when they protested, "Why have you brought all this trouble on your own people, Lord?" (Ex. 5:22).

God then responded with one of the most powerful paragraphs found in the Old Testament in Exodus 6:6–8. In short, He reminded them that indeed He was their God. Even if they couldn't see it, even if they couldn't understand His ways, He was freeing them. He was their God and could be trusted. Friend, we have an Enemy who wants us to live by what we can see, touch, and feel. Yet we have a God who calls us to live by faith. If we allow our discouragement over our frustrating circumstances to lead us into unbelief, then we will miss out on the upcoming miracles that God has in store for us.

God was *with* the Israelites. Pharaoh's harsh responses and defiance didn't surprise God. He was still in charge and His plan was still in place. Rest assured that is just as true today for us as it was for them! We must remember, however, that should He use measures to deliver us in ways we can't understand, and things get harder before they get better, we must choose to trust Him with it. God is with *us*.

Are you in the pit of some perceived reversal? Have you expected God to come through a little more quickly than He has? What does it look like for you to continue to trust Him while sitting in some disappointment?

BLESSINGS THROUGH CLOSE PROXIMITY

From the day Joseph was put in charge of his master's
household and property, the Lord began to bless Potiphar's
household for Joseph's sake. All his household affairs ran
smoothly, and his crops and livestock flourished.
Genesis 39:5 NLT

DID YOU KNOW THAT GOD CAN choose to bless others simply because they are within close proximity to you? It's true! In fact, we can see its recurring theme throughout Scripture. For example, "'Please listen to me,' Laban replied [when speaking to Jacob]. 'I have become wealthy, for the Lord has blessed me because of you'" (Gen. 30:27). How had Laban become wealthy? Because of his proximity to Jacob, one of God's children.

In today's Scripture, onsider Potiphar's household being blessed. Why did all of his household affairs run smoothly and his crops and livestock flourish? It was because God was blessing Joseph, and as a result Potiphar was blessed. Amazing.

We see it again when an angel told Paul not to be afraid during a terrible storm. "God in his goodness has granted safety to everyone sailing with you" (Acts 27:24 NLT). How had all those sailors and prisoners escaped harm when the ship eventually wrecked? It was because of their proximity to Paul, God's messenger.

As I read those passages, God makes it abundantly clear that He is not just all about you. In fact, one of His greatest desires is to reveal Himself to others through your life. Because He loves mankind so much and desires a relationship with each one of us, He goes out of His way bless those who come around His children. He wants others to know He is real and longs to demonstrate His very real presence to them. Does He have to do this? No. He just does it because He's good.

Do you want to be a conductor of the blessings God? Then do as Jacob, Joseph, and Paul did. Walk closely with Him. There is something powerful that happens inside a person who recognizes that others will be blessed as a direct result of their walking closely with God. It deepens our awareness that all good comes from Him and of our need to remain firmly attached to Him.

Have you ever experienced God's blessings in someone else's life that impacted yours simply because of your proximity to them? Does that change the way you think of how close you want to be to God?

COME OUT FROM DROWNING

*Keep me from lying to myself; give me the privilege of
knowing your instructions. I have chosen to be faithful;
I have determined to live by your regulations. I cling to
your laws. Lord, don't let me be put to shame!"*
Psalm 119:29–31 NLT

HAVE YOU EVER FELT EMOTIONALLY LOW? Like the kind of low that tempts
you to believe the lie that you're never going to feel happy ever
again? The kind of low that tempts you to believe your situation is
hopeless? I have. The reality is sometimes life's circumstances can
tempt us to believe the lie that we will never break through the
waves that are trying to submerge us.

The goal, however, is not to allow ourselves to be drowned
by our emotions or circumstances. So what can we do? How can
we stay afloat? Here are some ideas, and while some of them may
sound "churchy," they have served as life preservers during times
when I have felt like I was drowning.

First, as in the example provided in the Scripture above, we
must ask the Lord to help us to stop lying to ourselves. We need

to ask Jesus to help us discern between our thoughts about our circumstances versus His thoughts about them. We can begin this process by writing down on paper every lie we have believed thus far in one column and then writing the truth found in God's Word that demolishes that lie.

Second, we should pray even if we don't have the words. Jesus hears cry of our hearts. His response to His children's prayers has never been about our having perfect words. He hears the things we can't even bear to say out loud.

Third, we should worship. And I don't mean listening to any old song you can find on the radio. Those are fine, but when we are in a spritual battle, we need the kind of music that remind of God's power and strength. Worship that put the focus back on God's greatness! I call them battle songs. Songs that remind you that our God is a God who wins. Songs that remind you that He is always working even when we can't see or feel Him. Songs that remind us of the truth!

Finally, we should read our Bibles daily in order to remind ourselves that there isn't any situation that God cannot handle. It reminds us of God's power and of His presence. Often, meeting with a trusted friend or a Christian counselor is great for wrestling through some of our most gut-honest feelings.

I think it is easy to form a bad habit of not doing many of these things because we don't *feel* like doing them. The key is doing them anyway regardless of how we feel. Why? Because we need to come to the place of understanding that God is the only one powerful enough to turn our darkness into light. In fact, He is the One in whom "there is no darkness" (1 John 1:5). He helps us not to "lie to ourselves" and He reminds us that we do not need to feel any shame in bringing our brokenness to Him.

Have you discovered how easy it is to lie to yourself? What other ideas have helped you stay afloat when you've felt like you were drowning? What have you done to take responsibility for your own joy?

WHEN GRIEF BLURS
OUR SIGHT

My vision is blurred by grief.
Psalm 6:7 NLT

I THINK THE "BLURRED VISION OF grief" can come in many different forms. I'm sure you have experienced grief on different levels. The job was lost, the diagnosis heartbreaking, or the financial burden seem too great. Divorce papers were received. A dearly loved prodigal child persistently walks away from God's best for them. Like the agonized psalmist writes in Psalm 6, "I am worn out from my sobbing. All night I flood my bed with weeping, drenching it with my tears." We too have cried ourselves to sleep many nights believing nothing good will ever arise out of the ashes of our pain.

However, one of the things I am most grateful for is that we have a God who restores vision. Not only does He restore physical sight to the blind, but He also restores vision to our souls. The physical healing of sight is one thing, but if my inner man is blinded with grief, what hope do I have to ever see anything of value again?

There will always be things that seek to blind us and steal our vision. I don't know about you, but I need the Lord's vision in matters where I cannot see beyond my own grief. I must believe that when I turn my tear-stained face upward, He turns His loving face downward and wipes my face clean.

Second Corinthians 3:16 says, "But whenever someone turns to the Lord, the veil is taken away." When we fix our eyes on Jesus, He will remove the veil of grief and give us eyes to see again. Friend, the Lord has not stopped restoring your vision, and perhaps it's our time to give our soul blindness to Him for healing.

Have you ever been blinded by grief? What happened when you turned your tear-stained face to Jesus? Have you ever experienced His sort of restored vision of the soul?

SACRIFICING THE FUTURE INVESTMENT

"Look, I'm dying of starvation!" said Esau.
"What good is my birthright to me now?"
Genesis 25:32 NLT

ESAU AND JACOB WERE TWIN BROTHERS. Because Esau had been born first, he was first in line to receive a double share of the family's inheritance. But at this moment, he had just come in from the wilderness and was "exhausted and hungry." So hungry that when he smelled the stew his brother, Jacob, had been cooking, he exclaimed, "I'm starved! Give me some of that red stew!"

Jacob saw his brother's famished state as an opportunity to undermine his older brother's rightful position. He agreed to serve his older brother the savory dish he had cooked under one condition: that he be given the rights of the firstborn. Esau responded by saying that his birthright wasn't worth anything to him now because he was dying of starvation.

Many of us look at this story and think of how insane a person might be to trade their birthright for a bowl of stew. It appears that because was exhausted, starving, and smelled something delicious, he desired food more than his birthright. Unfortunately, this was the perfect setup for Esau to lose everything.

I wonder how many of us have given into what we wanted "right now" versus what was worth waiting for? Perhaps we spent time in the wilderness, came in exhausted from life, were weary in the wait, and found ourselves desiring all things of the flesh. We found it easy to sacrifice our future inheritance for our present cravings. And like Esau, we now carry the regret that comes with those whims.

I wonder if Esau spent much time wondering what would have been of his life had he not acted so rashly that day. I know I have wondered the same at different points in my own life. So if anything, this is what I know—if we don't want to spend the rest of our lives wondering what could have been, we must surrender what our desires are for right now, to the God who knows (and can be trusted with) our future. If we don't, surely we will give up the best that God has for us.

So take time to pray about your immediate desires and see if they square up with God's long-term goals for your life. Sometimes they do, and that's always fun. But sometimes they don't, and we must draw on God's strength to help us say no to the thing our flesh is screaming out for at the moment. Friend, the Lord's plans are always better than ours. Let's work to trust Him even when it feels impossible to do so. God's best will always be worth the wait.

Have you ever sacrificed a long-term goal for an immediate return? How did it turn out? How can you look to the Lord for the future?

CLIMBING THE WATCHTOWER

I will climb up to my watchtower and stand at my guard-post. There I will wait to see what the Lord says and how He will answer my complaint.

Habakkuk 2:1 NLT

I COMPLAIN TO GOD A LOT. I don't like to think it's complaining when I'm doing it, but if I'm being honest, I'm totally complaining. Sentences form on my lips like, "I hate this," "I wish this was different," or "old so-and-so is literally driving me crazy . . . again."

By the grace of God, however, not all of my prayers are selfish and self-centered complaints. Sometimes they are genuine requests that I know only God can answer. Like my friend who needs a miraculous healing from cancer or a friend whose marriage is being destroyed or another asking God for the wisdom required in parenting. I know I can bring all these things before Him and know He hears me.

Interestingly, when the prophet Habakkuk prayed, he went a step further and positioned himself to *receive the answers* to his prayers. In fact, the words *watchtower* and *guardpost* indicate how strongly he believed God would respond to his requests. You see, watchtowers were built into city walls and the watchmen would stand guard, scanning far into the distance to spot and ward off any approaching enemy so the city would be protected and not taken by surprise. Through prayer Habakkuk was climbing his watchtower to look far into the distance to see how and when God was going to respond to his requests.

So what about us? Are we positioning ourselves as readily as Habakkuk to hear the Lord's answers to our prayers? Or do we just run off a shopping list of wants and needs, returning to our days not really expecting any sort of real answer? Friend, we shouldn't be caught off guard when the Lord answers our prayer requests. We should be *expecting* it. Perhaps it is time to position ourselves like Habakkuk and climb to our watchtowers to see and receive our answers.

When you pray, do you believe God will answer? Why or why not?

ANCIENT FAITH

These are the nations that the LORD left in the land to test those Israelites who had not experienced the wars of Canaan. He did this to teach warfare to generations of Israelites who had no experience in battle. . . . These people were left to test the Israelites—to see whether they would obey the commands the LORD had given to their ancestors through Moses.

Judges 3:1–2, 4 NLT

I THINK WE WOULD ALL AGREE that seasons of testing are hard. Whether it is taking finals in school or being surprised by a pop quiz, testing isn't always a fun thing. The older I become, however, I have found that seasons of testing are much harder to pass when you feel like they are tied to life and death situations. Your marriage is on the rocks. The chemo isn't working. You were forced into early retirement. Admittedly the unscheduled tests of trusting God with the hardships of this life can rattle a person to the core. In fact, they don't feel much like a test but a very real battle in which we must stay alive.

The Lord knew this when He allowed the enemies of Israel to come against them. He wanted His people to know they could have victory if they obeyed the commands He had given them through their ancestors. His goal in testing was to teach them how to win their battles. It was to stretch them and to strengthen them and to build their faith in Him, not to destroy them. He intentionally allowed hard people, hard battles, and hard circumstances to come against the Israelites to grow their dependence on Him.

Friend, this is also what the Lord does with us. We cannot fight our battles with a secondhand faith held onto by our ancestors. We must learn to develop a firsthand faith to fight our own battles against hopelessness, fear, and overwhelming odds that come at us. We must remember that the things we so often want to rage against are the very things God wants to use to strengthen our faith in Him.

What are you doing to obey the commands God gives in His Word and pass those tests?

SHOWING UP ON TIME

*The Lord replies, "I have seen violence done to the helpless,
and I have heard the groans of the poor. Now I will rise
up to rescue them, as they have longed for me to do."*
Psalm 12:5 NLT

HAVE YOU EVER FELT AS IF the Lord hasn't shown up at the appropriate time for the struggles in your life? Perhaps you're like Martha in John 11:21, saying, "Lord, if only you had been here, my brother would not have died."

"If you had only been here." Can you hear the angst? Martha decided that if God had just shown up on her time schedule, her brother would have not died, and she would not be suffering.

From a human standpoint, I think it's totally understandable; however, God doesn't view time the same way humans do. In fact in the New Testament, two separate words, *chronos* and *kairos*, describe "time." *Chronos* is where we get the word *chronological* and describes time in past, present, and future tenses. *Kairos* describes an appointed time, and it's the moment that God's divine and purposeful movement interrupts the cosmos and something magnificent is accomplished. Some historians describe it in terms of archery, marking the exact time when an arrow is fired with enough force to break through its target.

Psalm 12:5 reassures us that while we may think God has left our prayers unanswered, we are misinformed by our emotions. The Lord is reminding us that He sees, He hears, and He "will rise up to rescue" us when His time is right. God knows exactly where His arrows of healing, deliverance, provision, and comfort need to hit in order to create a breakthrough. When He shoots, the arrows won't miss their target, nor will they fail to accomplish their mission.

We can all feel like Martha did regarding the illness and death of her brother. It's in those moments, however, we need to be reminded of the Lord's promises. If you know the story, Martha's brother was resurrected when Jesus finally did show up. Surely the Lord's cosmic timetable is better than ours even when we can't understand it. Release Him from your sense of *chronos* and trust Him to work within His *kairos*. Eventually you'll discover that He is always right on time.

Have you ever felt like Martha, thinking God just didn't show up in time? Does knowing the difference between *chronos* and *kairos* provide a deeper understanding of God's time frame versus yours?

WHEN LIGHT BREAKS THROUGH DEPRESSION

Then he [Elijah] went on alone into the wilderness,
traveling all day. He sat down under a solitary broom
tree and prayed that he might die. "I have had enough,
LORD," he said. "Take my life, for I am no better than my
ancestors who have already died."
1 Kings 19:4 NLT

ON MY DARKEST DAYS THE BIBLE reminds me that depression isn't a mark of weakness. I'm thankful that it is not ignored in Scripture. I am grateful that those who struggle against the darkness are not designated by God as people too broken to be used for the kingdom.

In fact, some of the greatest heroes of our faith struggled against feelings of despair:

Elijah asked God to "take his life" (1 Kings 19:4).
Paul was "crushed and overwhelmed, despaired of even life" (2 Cor. 1:8–9).

David described his soul as "downcast" (Ps. 42:11)

Jonah asked God to "take away my life," and was "angry enough to die" (Jonah 4:3,9)

Job said, "I loathe my very life" (Job 10:1)

Jeremiah said, "Cursed be the day I was born" (Jer. 20:14)

Even Jesus was described as "a man of sorrows, and acquainted with grief" (Isa. 53:3)

Any one of us who love God can still struggle with depression. We are not exempt from the feelings of emptiness that can come from this broken world. And in my own struggle, I have found this very unique gift inside depression's ugly wrapping. It can best be described as a very special and tender light that never goes out. I've discovered that it's the presence of God that never leaves me, and should I choose to focus on His light, it begins to brighten my world again.

Jesus said, "I am the light of the world. Whoever follows me will never walk in darkness, but will have the light of life" (John 8:12). If you find yourself sitting in darkness and you're wondering when the light will come into your life again, refocus on the Light of the World. For "this is the message we heard from Jesus and now declare to you: God is light, and there is no darkness in him at all" (1 John 1:5).

Light is always present, friend. Choose to set your gaze on His when you cannot find your own.

Have you considered depression as something that should disqualify you from serving God? When darkness wants to take over, how do you deliberately refocus on the Light of the World?

WHEN GOD ASKS THE IMPOSSIBLE OF US

Then the Lord told him, "Reach out and grab its tail." So Moses reached out and grabbed it, and it turned back into a shepherd's staff in his hand.

Exodus 4:4 NLT

IN THIS SCRIPTURE, MOSES HAD JUST been asked to throw his staff down before God. The Lord turned that rod into a snake as a sign to show His power to Moses. In the next verse, "Moses jumped back." I can assure you that jumping back would have been the least of my own responses. I would have run away from there as fast as my legs would carry me.

Interestingly, however, after Moses jumped back, he did just the opposite of what I would have done. He went on to do exactly as God had asked him to do, by picking up the snake and watching it turn right back into his shepherd's staff.

This is a clear reminder that not everything God asks of us will seem to make sense to us. Moreover, we may wonder if what He's asking of us shows any wisdom at all. Pick up a snake by the tail? No thank you. Forgive someone for embezzling from your company? Nope. Forgive your husband for having an affair? Forget it. Witness to the drunk driver who hit your loved one. Absolutely not.

But Moses did obey. He did the thing that didn't make sense. The thing that had first triggered a fear response. He obeyed God, and as a result of his obedience, Moses later experienced that same staff defeating Egypt's gods, separating the Red Sea, bringing water forth from a rock, and holding it up to achieve victory in battle. Perhaps what we see with Moses may just inspire us to trust what God is asking us to do. This is the life we really want, one marked by obedience to God so we can experience the miracles He has for us.

Have you ever felt like what God asked you to do seemed crazy at the time? What did He teach you through it? Is He asking you to trust Him with anything else today?

WHEN THE HEART CRIES

*I have wandered away like a lost sheep; come and find
me, for I have not forgotten your commands.*
Psalm 119:176 NLT

I THINK THIS IS ONE OF the sweetest and most authentic heart cries in all of Scripture. I can hear the writer literally pouring his heart out in prayer, devastated by his lostness. "I don't even think I can find my way home anymore. I've made so many mistakes along the way. I'm depressed. I can't get out of bed. My friends have left me. My family has rejected me. I know that when I was a child I was raised to know You. I remember people pointing me to You. I remember Sunday school teachers teaching me about You. My parents loved You, my grandparents served You, but I'm an adult now, and I'm just so lost. Would You just please come and find me? I don't know where to find You."

Isn't that just the most honest thing? Admitting that we've wandered away from God? Telling Him that we need help coming home again? I believe this is why Jesus brought up the question in Matthew 18:12–13, "If a man has a hundred sheep and one of them wanders away, what will he do? Won't he leave the ninety-nine others on the hills and go out to search for the one that is lost? And if he finds it, I tell you the truth, he will rejoice over it more than over the ninety-nine that didn't wander away!"

Jesus wants to come and gather up those who cry out to Him to be found. He rejoices to come to them. If you're lost today, stop trying so hard to find your own way home. Instead, call out for Jesus to come to find you. You aren't lost to Him. Rest assured, He knows exactly where to find you.

Have you ever felt like you had wandered so far away from God you were sure He had no idea where you were? How does it comfort you to know that He has never lost sight of you?

ORDER INFORMATION

REDEMPTION
P R E S S

To order additional copies of this book, please visit
www.redemption-press.com.

Also available on Amazon.com and BarnesandNoble.com
or by calling toll-free 1-844-2REDEEM.